PEN OF LOVE, FROM THE HONEY-DEW OF HEART..... STORY OF AMRAPALI...

AKS DEEP (KUNTAL GHOSH)

ISBN 979-888606198-7

As it's my first collection of poems,
I have to sent a million of thank you rehoboams,
Please bear with my flow of with low hums,
First I want to thank my sisters for their inspiration,
My teachers for inculcating in me the love for reading and expression.
My lovely friend, Rumki,a real pickel pie,
For being my teacher,my rectifier instead of my admire,thy.
Than the platter of poets I have read from Keats to Rabindranath,
From Madhusudan to Wordsworth,
From Shahir to Muntashir,
From Harivansh to Kumar Vishwas,
From Kalidas to Kabir,
From Tulsidas to Bulley Shah,
From Amrita Pritam to many more whom my brain presently can't recall,
I want to put a toast of thanks to all.
And finally I bow down in reverence to two,
Without whom I would never have been Aks Deep from Kuntal.
My grandfather and Ramdhari Singh Dhinkar,
My grandfather in his youth was use to doing theater,
And his awards and stories have made me lure to become Aks Deep from Kuntal.
And Ramdhari Singh Dhinkar has given Aks Deep his breath, yaha,

He is to me, same as, Drona was to Ekalvya.

His master-piece Rashmirathi and Parashuram ki pratiksha has given Aks Deep the words,
And his poetry Urvashi gave Aks Deep the love of expressions.
So I will start by bowing down in gratitude to the Adi-yogi's glorious feets....

Contents

Contents

Contents

If You Love, Love Like Shiv

As through this collection I want to talk of love ooze,
So,I surrender my ignorant self turpitude,
And my vocab and brain in his ultimate servitude.
I surrender myself before that Adi yogi,
The true epitome of love,
Who obstinate in love,
Gave everyone a shove.
But he never tried to be a love-dove of express,
Or tried to impress.
But the whole world has seen that it was the emotions of love that have bounded him to calmness,
And the same emotion of love made him the destructive violence.
The whole world has witnessed, for Sati his alluring adamant devotion.
Sati died, with her ash,it seemed his emotions all died,and washed off,
He becomes violent and than calm,
And finally he waited for Shakti for eras to come.
Probably he was the inspiration of Ram,
To cross every border in love that this brain has ever thought to cram.
So says the Prithvi,
If you love, than in love, no unaltered stone you leave,

And says the time,
If you love, love like Shiv
In love you may not be present during the brightest of days
But promise yourself,
That for love you will always be there during the stromiest of the nights.
So says the time,
If you love, love like Shiv....

Preface

As this books is my poetic collecton of love. So I can't stop myslef from sharing three of my favourite dohes of Kabir:

"ऐसी वाणी बोलिए, मन का आपा खोय |
औरन को शीतल करे, आपहु शीतल होय ||"

In this couplet,how beautifuly he expresses the lovely words. He says that there can never be a bitter weapon than word that can crush hearts, and there can't be anything as lovely as words than make one's brain calm and can also make other's happy and calm.

"चिंता ऐसी डाकिनी, काट कलेजा खाए |
वैद बेचारा क्या करे, कहा तक दवा लगाए ||"

In this couplet, how beautifully he expresses the love towards inner peace, he says that worry is such awitch which feeds on our heart and destroies our peace, how can even doctor prescribe a medicine to it.

But he has himself answered the medicine to it.

दुख: में सुमिरन सब करे, सुख में करे न कोई ।
जो सुख में सुमिरन करे, तो दु:ख काहे को होय ॥

In this couplet, how beautifully he expressed love towards lord, he says that in distress everyone of us remember him, but if we remember him everytime that agony and sarrow and worry cannot touch us even.

रहिमन धागा प्रेम का , मत तोरो चटकाय |
टूटे पे फिर ना जुरे, जुरे गाँठ परी जाय ||

In this couplet, how beautifully he explains sincerity of love, he says love is like athin thread of our soul, once it's broken you have to tie it up to re-mend it, but every time we try to re-mend it gets screwed up being entangled.

"बुरा जो देखन मैं चला, बुरा न मिलिया कोय।
जो दिल खोजा आपना, मुझसे बुरा न कोय।।"

Finally in this couplet how beautifully he express to makae ourself better and I belive without a better ourselve we can never be the ultimate lover, so how beautifully he explains it here, I roamed everywhere in search of bad, but I can never find any, but when I look inside myself, I found there can never be a worse person like me.

Prologue

I would love to share the poem of Bulley Shah, because beside the love of Shiva this poem has inspired me to make this compilation:

"zeher vekh ke pita ta ki pita,
ishq soch ke kita te ki kita,
dil de ke je dil len di aas rakhi,
o ha! bulleya, pyar eho jeha kita te ki kita! ! !"
Here he says, " You call youreslf brave,
But want to have a look at the poison before you have it,
Are you even brave,
(It show reminds me of Socrates)
Bulley goes on to say, "You thought of love and loved,
Than was it even love,
You in love gave someone your heart,
But in return you expected a heart full of love back from her, Was that even love or a bargain..."

In just this few lines how beautifully he epressed true love, that was the beauty of Bulley Shah, like the sands of of the soil of thar to which he belonged, his poems are everlasting source of knowledge dipping with unbearably-gorgeous sense of life caramalized in intolerably-alluring simplicity....

1. You and me in the game of Time

What an amazing game,
This unbearably-beautiful time has played,
Nither you could be you,
Nor I could be I.
The tome that we called love,
Was just a shadow of complying-commerce.
I knocked this world off,
In just one confidence of love,
That was you.
But you never had the credence over love,
You never had the conviction,
Nither on me, nor on you, nor on the love.
Now, I just have one confussion,
That play it's violin in this heart,
You sometime said, "Love",
Was the fable a romance,
Or just a flicker of emotions.
But probably those passing seconds could have been smitten,
That has just passed by as my trial of love,
If those hours had not been forbidden and forlorn,

Those hours could have been love,

What an amazing game,

This unbearably-beautiful time has played,

Nither you remained you,

Nor I could be I.....

2. Obsession of "Yourself"

Being so much obsessed by yourself,
Being so much encaged in yourself,
Being so much possessed by yourself,
How can you even love yourself,
.Being so much occupied by yourself.....

3. Cheap-expensive love (A thanks giving note to the chocolate-companies)

In this choclate day,
I want to gift a bouquet of chocolate to you all with utmost love of affray,
Thank you for making us unhealthy with a bar load with sugars,
Thank you for your advertisement that made our emotions as cheap as lures,
Equivalent to a bar of sugar that we call choclates.
Thank you for your promotions that made our emotions go down and down and
the cost of your bar with loads of sugar go up and up,
Than the dark chocolate joins the club.
Thank you for your dark chocolate and it's build up.
Thanks for making it a status symbol,
The girl and boy who adds two full spoon of sugar into their tea and coffee in a nimbel,
Started saying I love dark chocolates like the music of the kimbel.
After-all how can one plunder their status in the societies duel.
Thanks for making emotions so costly-cheap,
That only some currency can buy but not the soul can reap.

Thanks for creating this beautiful world where the sweets are consider,
A calorie bumper ,
Dismantling the modern concept of diet siddur,
But not so your bar loaded with sugars do it's trendier,
Thanks for all this,dear.
And specially making emotions like love
Cheap enough to be bought with some currency thereof,
Because everyone can't afford a costly heart hereof.
Thanks to you all for making love a synonym of your caramelized sugar coated bar,
Thanks for this cheap-expensive love,dear
Because in today's world most of us can't afford a costly heart, it's very rare.....

4. Proposal

If I would have loved you,
I could have proposed you,
But fortunately or unfortunately my soul loves your's,
Do it have any control of propose,
Isn't they outside the bounds of request, rejection and acceptance....

5. Rose Day

Once a girl asked me, "You must be saving few bucks this day?
As you are out of this game of heart which they call valentine day."
I answered with a smile, "Why do you think so??"
She said with a palatial wink, "You don't have to buy roses, to bestow?"
I said with a big smile, "Who said you so?? I have to buy a bouquet, you know."
She gazed at me,
I started with a glory smile, "A purple one for this gift of world filled with passion and infatuation,
A burgundy in the lord almighty's devotion,
A red for love and admiration,
For every beautiful thing that God has gifted in abounds ,
Lavender for the unique love that we have for life surrounds,
A pink for the attitude of gratitude for every beautiful things arounds,
White for the innocence that resides with beauty confounds,
Yellow for the charming friendship's bounds...."
She gives a sigh and stops me, "Ok, Ok fine...is in that bouquet,there any rose for humans like us.."
She says with a winky dimple,

I said with a smile jiggle, "Just a sec, "
She looks at me stunned,jittles peck.
While I bought the bouquet from the near by rose shop and gifted her the rosy deck.
She was perplexed her mouth opens up wide, "What the hecks?"
I closed it so that no flies get in or the butterfly of his surprise fluttering in her heart don't out gets.
And I said, "A purple one for being with me and push me for my passion even when this whole world disbelived me,
For being a patient teacher improving my speech-bee,
Guru Brahma, Guru Vishnu, Guru Deva Maheshwara, Guru sakshat parambrahm tasmāye sri guruvai namaha..so this burgundy one for thee,
A red for the love and admiration of friendship because you are one of the best gift God have given me.
Lavender for the unique love of yours that takes me out of tough situation's rust,
Pink for always being for me and holding me up with your love and words and pull me up whenever I feel downcast.
White for your innocence, natkhat,
And the yellow for always being my best friend and my best part... "
She makes her eyes as round as the full moon and smacked my hand with a smile,
The girl is no-one but my best-friend of all times,my sister my life's gaiety isle ...

6. Small love stories

Meeting with a smiling face,
And leaving in agony and angers embrace,
And between these lies million small love stories tangeled lace,
Sonets of unkown love and known pains,
Often than not at the end of these journeys,
Says the heart, "Sometime it's better to remain stranger,
Than these journey of becoming known, than friend and than stranger again in lone".......

7. Teddy bear, teddy bear how did you came into being?

With some drench of Theodore Roosevelt as the story ring,
With some funny-pinch of jovial sting.
What!!!it had the president involved??
So, you had been famous from the very first day you have evolved.
May be so.
Hey please share the story as it go.
The story is short,
It's like this, a funny stot.
It was 1902 Teddy, oh whom you called Theodor Roosevelt,decided,
To hunt, and he will hunt only a bear, he confirmed.
But as luck has it he couldn't hunt a bear,
Even he can't see one, bear seemed very rare.
It was eve, so thought the Mississippi town,
How can the president's head be laid down.
So they caught a bear and kept it tied,
And the president they invited.
Teddy came but didn't shoot the bullet,

He refuse to kill the bear, he says, "how cute is this bear with his tummy chubby gullet."

He walks off,

And next day the Washington post goes round with a picture with a beautiful scoff,

"Teddy, refused to kill the bear cutie."

From there through the mind of Steiff I came into being like this cootie,

And this is how I came into the toys, movies and other rings of tutti.

Cool, and than you became this hooty.....

8. Why did you?

If you wanted to incapacitate I,
You should have made me cry,
Why did you blemish my isle?
After making me smile.....

9. WhatsApp, valentine and a soldier...

There stands a soldier in the hedged snow of Siachen,
The snow-cladded wind penetrating, his coat giving him ice sponge at -40,
The snow-capped peaks gazing at him,
His fingers turning stiff as stiff as wood under the burden of national-security midst thess Galgan.
His eyes are transfixed over the mobile screen,
There is a message of his wife popping out of the rim.
It reads, "My dear valentine, I love you,
I don't say it out of habit,
I say it to remind you that a part of my heart is with you,inhabit.
I miss you whenever I am tossing in this empty bed,
I miss your hot-breath of affection in every wind blowing in this big empty room like the dead,
Touch of sentiment in every cress of this empty sheet in dread."
The soldier's eye get filled with emotion making his eyes gloomy,
But it was just for a second of doomy,
He looks up his shoulder into the Indian flag smiling at him in high,

He smiles and salute at it in reply.
And writes, "Dear I love you too from the bottom of my heart,
But there are many threads of sorrow in this world other-than love tart,
There are many comforts in this world to yearn for other-than our passionate-union,
There are million of wish in this heart other-than living in your embrace communion,
Million of desire to die for other-than dying in your lap."
He ends it up with an emoji of Indian flag.
That was enough to carry his emotions to his belove,
She replies it with an emoji of love and salute glove.
Soon a beautiful smile floods his lip,
Midst all this snow taking the reading of thermometer down trip,
He can feel the warm-embrace of affection and love of his wife's grip,
Squeezed between his love for the Indian flag from the very heart's deep...

10. Valentine

You are the moon,
You are the sun,
You are the firy palm,
You are the calm,
You are the rock pillar,
And no failure.
You are the delicate flower of grace,
You are inspirational embrace,
You are love,
You are the blazing dove,
My best friend, My majesty, My pickel Pie,My cloud nine,
A very happy valentine...

11. Small peg of love

Isn't it the small things,
That mean more than anything,
The simple glee,
That make a heart beat flee,
The breathe of a flower,
Or the grace of heavenly shower.
The aroma of a empty path underneath a sky desolate,
That fill lungs,makes the agony and the anguish obsolete,
The horizon and the embrace of someone's words of love narrate.
Turns the world back from the upside down again
Brings a nourishing reason to be alive again,
Isn't this love,
Small yet the most intolerably-beautiful peg of love....

12. A love letter to the reflection

A letter to that alluring reflection of gorgeousness,
Some words in name of my untamed desireness.
I want to meet you,
I also want to enjoy getting lost in untempt reminisce of you,
What's your name ?I don't know,
Where do you live ?I don't know,
But I know you are there??
And if you are there,
You will also have a name too,
But I want to clear you are not my obsessation hue,
And you are not in my memories strew,
Because this beautiful,is part of my tomorrow,doo.
While memories are a collection of hours that have gone by,
But you are my tomorrow's aby,
Or maybe of a day after, or a month after or after a year and few due.
But I want to meet you, and I am sure I will meet you,
I also want to enjoy getting lost in untempt reminisce of you.
Do you also think about me a lot?
Do I also come into your thought,

As a nameless twilight brought,
As an indefinite face caught,
And you only know about my ought??
I want to meet you,
I also want to enjoy getting lost in untempt reminisce of you....

13. Lessons

Life had made me cry so much,
That I have learnt to laugh even when my heart was drenched in tears and search,
The time has injured me so many times in it's tests,
That I learnt the enjoyment of fight,getting out of the mode of requests..

14. Memories- dreams dense

This poor heart have said allured in dreams dense,
Saturated in the wine of sense,
It's love for you is so intense,
He is not very happy even when you yourself have came,
He have that claim,
More than you,your memories are his love's devine flame.
Because when you will come,
You will talking of going making this heart numb,
The heart says he doesn't like it and says,"If in love,you want to be stubborn become,
Don't be stubborn to come or be stubborn to go,
But be obstinate to stay and never sucumb and together grow...

15. To the Ex- I don't hate...

To the Ex- I don't hate,
Why should I hate?
She wasn't just a fleeting flirting sensation,
But the depth of my oceanic emotion.
I have loved her,
Not made a bargain with her,
In love she responded she resounded,
Now she receded.
But why should that decrease my love and respect for her,
It was love not a passing vehemence to disappear.
It's on her to walk along or move back a slide,
But in my heart she will always reside.
Happiness is what I wish for her to dictate,
To the Ex I don't hate,
Why should I hate?
She wasn't just a passing flirting sensation,
But the oceanic depth of my emotion,
Just few things hurts me often.
She is so emotional,
She gets angry in so hasty motional.

Now when she gets angry mound,
Do anyone calm her down round,
With the affection she deserves abound?
She is so sweet like a child,
She often gets sulked up in small small things a wild.
Just it worries me when she is sulked up unnerves,
Than do anyone console her with the utmost love that she deserves?
She is like the impetuous adorable kid,
She needs someone to hold her up whenever she is about to break down in undid,
And thus finally it worries me when she is about to break down arid,
Is there anyone there with her to hold her up with utmost care and affection stringed?
This are the few things that make me worries,
But probably she is happy because she is away even from my flurries.
And I wish to God all happiness and for her only happiness to create,
To the Ex- I don't hate....

16. Valentine's Day

Once a girl asked me, "Why don't you celebrate valentine's day?"
I answered with a smile, "Because this day reminds me of
someone very close died and now down it lay."
She asked me, "Who?"
I answered with a malicious smile, "My heart whose burnt ash I
carry,still I carry it's strew,
Soaked in that lost honey-dew,
Which I thought was my valentine too..."

17. Why should you enjoy their jealousy??

They are jealous of you,
They wonder where do your secret lies.
You aren't cut for the society
Or to fit into some ordinary story.
You are a novel too precious of a bundle,
That they can afford or handle.
So when you start to tell them,
They think you're telling lies than.
They don't have the spirits,
To imagine those highs.
Whenever they ask,
Say to them
The sky is in the reach of yours arm.
You can breathe in the fresh air,
Put your mind at ease,
Let down your hair,
Let it flow in the breeze.
When they are trying to perfecting their looks,
Encasing themselves into their own cages rooks.
While you are the free bird who loves life with its flaws and

nooks.

You let your eyes wander,

To all the beauty to be seen in splendor.

If those toxic thoughts you still do ponder,

You let out a scream of thunder.

Scream until the pain is gone,

Until you no longer feel afraid of that nasty song.

Open your eyes to a new dawn,

Let the darkness fade out and be gone.

While they hide their inner soul,

In their hunt to be fit for the society's role,

They loose themselves everyday bit by bit in that parole,

While you focus on your goals.

You never lose your fight.

While they give up in the plight,

Instead of being tight.

You are the phenomenal women,

They can't be close to the synonym,

They are jealous of you,

They wonder where your secret lies.

They try so much,

But they can't touch,

Your inner mystery nor can ignore that,

The eyes to see it they lack,

Nor they have the sense to perceive that.

They are jealous of you

They wonder where your secret lies.

It's in the arch of your back,
In the glow of your smile that never lack,
The passion of your eyes.
The grace of your styles.
You are a woman Phenomenally.
Phenomenal woman, That's you.
Now you understand,
Just why they want your head's to bow,
Why they are judging you dow.
Why they are grudging on you?
They are jealous of you.
Which they will always be
For they can never be
They wonder where your secret lies.
You don't shout or jump about
Or have to talk real loud.
But that confidence
In the click of your heels,
The bend of your hairs,
The palm of your hands,
Makes them envy and want you to budge drowns,
'Cause you are a woman
Phenomenally.
Phenomenal woman, That's you,
That they can never be,
They are jealous of you,
They wonder where your secret lies.

An image unmatch

To hide their fear they want you to budge

'Cause you are a woman

Phenomenally.

Phenomenal woman, That's you,

That they can never be....

18. Aren't we all perfect

You wish you were perfect,
By the standards the society has set,
But is it worth it?
Just learn to love yourself,
Yaha that could take some time to love thyself.
You need not to stop dreaming,
And just let your thoughts flowing.
Stop trying to be perfect,
And let your dreams flow direct.
Sometimes life has its twists and turns,
You just have to find your charns,
Remember you are the best,
No matter what says the rest.
Though some people will try to tear your confidence down,
You have to get up around.
That's there for the cleanup pound.
You wish you were perfect,
But you're everything and more,beautifully erect,
And sometimes when you feel tied down,
You just need to spread your wings and soar abound....

19. Are we liberated?

Are we liberated??
Are we free??
We should ask ourselves, Have we attained freedom??
Are we liberated even or it's just a dumb??
We still fall for Macaulay's education system,
The police system is still the one that British has left behind the scum,
We still carry those rags adding sum,
It's been more than 70years but we have changed things very seldom.
It's the land where even views of people like Curzon have changed thee,
"India is a country of jugglar and Soccers",says he when he starts of his spree,
Meets Kena Ram Baba and than says Curzon,"East is a University where Scholars never get degree."
Still education of that country is judged on the parameters of grading scales they have set,
Still today soul-less education flourishes that to rule us they have made.
Still our eyes are shut for the old interactive beautiful education system,

Books like Panchantra which teaches the children every lessons of life has been put in the grave of the school librarys wisdom.
While books flourish that are im-moral,
With stories that are very trivial.
Throughout the world, there are thousands of colleges where Vedas are being studied and followed,
As a step to move forward in the advance science road,
While we ignore them and want them abandoned
The culture and essence of our country is dying and we silently say we are independent,
Are we liberated are we free or loving this brain being dominated?
This is a country where anexer like Alexander comes,
Meets Dandin and understand what's true liberation is,
He says in his dying anecdote to his soldiers,
"When you carry my dead-body let my hands be open and hanging from the coffin's very sides,
Showing the world that this materialistic empire capitalism is just the illusion's bind,
If you are ascended under the control of your senses you are leaving this world empty handed and blind.
This is the soil where Buddha earns Nirvana,
Narendra becomes Swami Vivekananda,
Vardhaman becomes Mahavira,
Ibrahim Khan becomes Ras Khan,
Where we had linage of Sanyashis,
The men who escape the bondage of indriyas

And is ruled by consciousness.
In this same-land we have become so materialistic that now riches,is determined by the bands of shoes and specs,
It sorrows me to see in this land this change,
To what has it became.
Where Mahavir and Buddha were considered far more rich than any king,
Where the king didn't made luxurious palace but spent time in development of people and their being,
To now where showing-off houses has become a common practice of sync.
We were the land from where a man wearing Saffron tunic went
In Chicago and showed the whole world what ultimate salvation and enjoyment meant.
And now we are getting more and more bounded to the brands and these materialistic goal
Are we even liberated from the colonial rule or is it now even dictating our soul.
Vipasana changed into Vasana,
Are we liberated from the colonial education system,
Or falling more and more for it falling prey to the market of the west's esteem,
Selling us materials by diminishing ourselves from within.
Vedas is considered the most scientific textbook by the world
Thus culture that followed it was scientifically far ahead of us as it have whirled,
MIT have been using Sanskrit as a high-level output language

from Quantum computers efficacy,
Due to its less spin-polarised q-bits storage efficiency.
While we look down on it,
Einstein to Oppenheimer everyone tried to dip in the ocean of Vedas in search of the pearl of knowledge fit.
We have encased our knowledge and thoughts in those strong chain of Macaulay's education manifesto,
How can we enjoy freedom unless our mind isn't freed of the English education system that was made to rule us through and through.
Unless we don't break ourselves free from the bondage of this colonial realm,
Can our souls be liberated like the helm.
Can we enjoy complete freedom or Purna Swaraj,
When we are becoming more and more caged up
And chained by the Union Jack.
We need not be ruled always physically,
When our mind is ruled by them superfluously.
Are we enjoying any status better than Dominion-status,
We follow their police rule and there stratus,
Their rule of judiciary,
Their education system binary,
And making English more than a language a superiority.
I don't find any country in the world,
Who follows the administration policies and other rules of their ruler after becoming independent with herld,
It's just has engaged us within that colonial rule that within us

we still withhold.
Making our soul and brain less and less independent with every passing year in the spree,
Earlier our body was caged in the shackles of slavery,
While our soul and brain was liberated and free.
Now we may look physically free but our soul and brain is chained by subservience,
We should talk to ourselves, is this freedom even?
Is this for what our freedom fighters laid their life,
Jut for a dominion status to abide.
Or was it purna swaraj complete independence.
I put this question in front of our surveillance.
Are we liberated? Are we free??

20. You should never marry her whom you love....

You should love someone,
Whose acceptance is not accepted by the fate,
Because if you get the love,
Than it don't take even months before it diminishes it shades.
And if you get married to the person with whom you have loved inductance,
Then those yearning and longing of affection and love is lost in reluctance,
And finally the success of love seems like a tragic accidence....

21. Taj Mahal

Whenever we talk of love,
Everyone talks of Taj Mahal as an embodiment of love,
But is it love, is love so cheap drove?
Is love just a buisness of an Emperor,
Buying few names for him in this market of time'sc charter,
With the riches that he has collected and sucked off,
Making this just a big damn structure.
Made of white marble that shines like rubby-red,
Soaked in bloods and tears of those poor chopped-off hands dread.
It's not the corridor of love,
It's just a design of show-off of highest order of cove.
The air around these cadaver of love,
Is filled with cries of few voiceless hands of stockdove.
It's just the curtain of love behind which lust plays his music and tone,
Even the house of those dishonoured poets is better than this graveyard of white stone,
Whose city of words is soaked in the wine of love and permeate moan.
In that magnificent garden of the emperor,
What's the value of love of common peoples like us, Is it even

worthy more than a trash paper??
In that court the value of our love,
Is nothing more than those leaves lying on the carpet to be cleaned and out drove.
So let's we too say a good bye to this architect grandeaur of marbels,
And find for ourselve some corner in those almirahs of cobbles,
Behind those book where the infamou sonats of love harbours.
Let find ourselves a place where there is a meeting of dishonourable poets like us,
Where there is no show off of affection,
Nor any cloud of lavishness reflection,
But only are there tears drenched in warmth of intimacy or any pomp of expectance.....

22. Than it's better

If this broken heart shatters completely,
Than it's better.
If the destiny of this night becomes embellished,
Than it's better.
As few pauses and moments of intimacy and solace has passed with you,
If the remaining breaths also passes away in your lap,
Than it's better.
Before these audience which we call world,
What's good, what's bad??
If this heart can escape this,
Than it's better.
In truth it's you, who have destroyed me,
But if someone else could be blamed,
Than it's better....

23. Flexile but not Fragile

Be gentle, resilient, flexible not breakable.
It's life may be you loose at times,
You are not destined to win every time,
But remember you aren't a loser.
You are a wreck,
Even the best of ship also wreck,
But is remend,
So will you,you are just wrecked not totalled.
You are fractured,
Even a bone is fractured but with time it rejoins,much stronger,
So will you.
Keep the flare in you burning,
And your wills high rising,
You are just fractured not broken and will agin surely have an uprising.
You have failed,
Everyone fails now and again,
Just rise up you arn't a failure, damn.
It's time and tide that has flipped the coin just try a bit harder,
You may have fallen hard but can get up again more brawnyer.
This made you isolated,
And that made you free.

You are destroyed for a fresh rebuild,thee.

For time your heart is broken,

But it will be strongly mend again.

No matter how close you come to breaking,

Just be flexible to bend,not break.

Time and tide will take it's turns,

And you will win no matter what happens.....

24. A dream

Last night I saw a dream,
A dream sweet enough teaching the very essence of life,
It called me to hold fast on to it and clings,
I could see a bird with broken wings,
My eyes opened but I could see what I have just seen,
I understood why should I hold on to the dream??
For if dreams die,
Life is a broken-winged bird in the sky,
That cannot fly.
Why should I hold fast to dreams?
For when dreams go,
Life is a barren field dough,
Frozen with snow.....

25. She was my love and not oppressive attraction

In the sky of love million of my wishes had their wings spread out,
But never wanted to cage her or lock her in the name of love stout,
She was my love adoration,
And not a high-handness of oppressive attraction.
This heart knows,she can never be mine,
But still it has unshakeable faith that it will never forget her, she is the shrine,
And will never beat in the same way for some other,than thine.
Because she was my love adoration,
And not a high-handness of oppressive attraction...

26. It's not your fault

You thought love to be a game,
While I in the other hand devasted my life in just one faith that's love it's name.
But it's not your fault to plumbs,
Those lanes had an infamous repute among the crowded scrums,
But it was my naughty heart that fell head on for those houses in there some.
But just a small request of duction,
Don't disgrace me any further with the smile of destruction,
I have already been honoured with the title of 'unfaithful",on falling heels on in love for you and in your affection....

27. What's wrong with my heart??

The suitor says, "When the heart breaks than even the breath of life chokes."
The era says, "When your love is angry than even the time seems to be treacherous rouges."
The world says, "Every face has a mask, every damn one is perfidious and faithless."
The book says, "On hearing her no, the time seems to stop,heart seems to be motionless."
But I don't know what's wrong with my heart to do,
It just stopped on hearing her reply, "I love you too"....

28. Question to love

Who can stand up?
And can walk away from your encast,
Not being harrased,
Without cinders of past?
Why whom you touch,
Who falls under you clutch,
Always dries up a bit as such?
Why?Why??Why???
Isn't this is the why you look so alluring?
When with utter honesty you are lying.
Isn't it?Isn't it??Isn't it???

29. A Cocktail of friendship and fiance

Friendship is like the wine,
We drink it slow,
It's mischievous though,
We enjoy wholly in it's embrace and grow,
Through out the life it flow.
Fiance is most of the time like the hot can of beer,
We gulf it fast,
Often more than not, it doesn't last.
So let love also be a slow toast,
Remember it's the old champagne that we love the most,
Because in the winery of time it has roast.....

30. I can still cry like a baby

Catch my hand,
I can still be yours.
The wave of people are too much in a strand,
I can get lost in this crowd detours.
I could have also be the fore-runner in these race of world,
But moments reminds me of those friends that lagged back in times unfurled.
Even in this adult of me there still resides a child, it hadn't die,
Who can cry, even in small small things who can cry,
Who can still cry.....

31. Let's love be love, only love

Let's love be love, only love,
Nothing more, nothing less,
Nothing sweet, nothing spicy,
Nothing fresh, nothing messy,
Nothing economic,nothing grandeaur,
Nothing dark, nothing fair,
Nothing unsavoury, nothing delectable,
Let's love be love, only love, and lovable.....

32. Ultimate love

Time can be fast,
Time can be slow,
Time can go high,
Time can go low.
But it never stops it's flow casts,
And always lasts.
There's time for life,
There's time for final bed of quiet.
The intelligent-jester tries to time travel,
While the halfwit-clever tries to hold on to time's bubble,
While it's the empty vessel of light that lives and enjoy it's cavel and ravel.
Time is always right and bright,
It's the ratha kalpana that can be false and night.
The duck puddles and become the feast of the whirlpool,
While the swan drinks the milk from that same pool.
Having a beautiful jantar mantar of chrysanthemum is always an amazing soup of madness, happiness, sadness.
He is only happy,who knows,
Only thing that's permanent is the dial close,
And the three hands,one long, one medium and one short all together those.

And let himself flow in that blow without being hasty,
Some spends,while some saves,but at the end the bank is always empty.
Time wakes,
Time sleeps,
Time for spare is for care.
And that's what count,
Because at the end that's what comes back round,
When the rope is thrown at your neck to bound,
Sinking you down to the heaven of hound,
Underneath the ground echoing with ghastly sound.
Only thing that holds on to you making you bright and grand,
Is the petals that you have saved in that locker of sand.
Finally the ultimate love is crud that thud,
The diamond is covered with mud....

33. Amrapali- a journey from this world of senses to the abode of consciousness

Amrapali a journey from 'nagar-badhu' to 'bhikkhuni'.
Her journey from the very embrace of the supreme world of senses,
To the abode of ultimate consciousness.
Always had me intrigue,
So, I am weitting this poetic infringe.
Born around 600-500 BC on which many might up a question of disagree,
But over the story and the beauty of her transformation to the path of chetna
from this world, a slavery of senses, no one can deny or vary.
Her journey from the boundary of sense to consciousness,
Isn't it the ultimate love from histories bury.
Isn't the devotion for the lord almighty and his reflection in our soul
The ultimate cherishing love cherry.

Birth of the maiden in the garden mango laden

Birth of Amrapali,
The story starts with a person named Mahanaman,a Kama-deva's devote.
He finds a child in the lap of the mango garden,
Lured by his kamna of becoming father very ardent,
He adopted the girl and his own kingdom he abandoned.
He sets up residence in Ambara village, a small hamlet in Vaishali,
To protect her daughter from the evil eyes of his enemies and the lust-packed follys,
He named her 'Amrapali',
As he had found her under a mango tree in the royal gardens of Vaishali.

(Etymologically speaking, the name is derived from the two roots, "*Amra*" (meaning mango) and "*Pallawa*" (meaning tiny sprouts or leaves) so was he named Amrapali.)

Pleasent-unpleasent beauty

As expected, Amrapali grew up to be a woman of unfathomed
beauty esteem,
A womwn of extraordinary grace and charms intolerable-extreme.
She became famous in the entire city of Vaishali for her looks and
had a long legion,
Was declared as the most beautiful girl in the region,
At even in the tender age of eleven.
She became almost of all the growing boys dream,
As she grew older, many young nobles desired to spend time in her
alluring stream.
In order to avoid her suitors confrontation,
She was then bestowed the status of being Vaishali's state
courtesan.

Curse of beauty-lure of lust

Manudev, the King of Vaishali,
Once watched her performance in the city, was shaken by her overpowering lalique,
Couldn't escape her beauty.
He wished to have her for himself,
And hold the beauty in his nympholepsy embrace.
Amrapali looked ravisingly sweet in her blue saree, the king's depraved eye's chase.
Hugging her waist was a beautiful gold lace,
Which was complemented by a ruby necklace.
Manudev caught Amarpali's ivory like waist and pulled her to himself
And said, "I would have so loved to be your necklace or the lace,
Always getting a touch of your smooth ghee like flesh.
You look like a ravishingly beautiful angel,
Your smile is too gorgeous to handle.
Insanely cute face,
Mesmerizing killer eyes that's making me attract to you like glue and your unbearable grace.
Just a drop-dead effigy of beauty,
Every queen and princess would be jealous of you darling, sweety.
You really look like an mammon image of beauty with a brain,
Those waves of your waist are enough to swerve me off my feet

like a man slips in rain.

Your smile is infectious, those large brown eyes are hypnotizing me,

Your ivory waist had curves of softness thee.

The black hair falling brilliantly over your chest,

Dazzles as your body turns elegantly making me so obsessed.

The hair caressing the curves has mesmerised me in the way,

Like the earth is mesmerized by the first drops of rain after a hot scorching day."

Arrogant and inconsiderate about her feelings he tried to kiss her.

Amrapali got very annoyed with it as she with force shake the king, the salacious vivre,

Escaping from his squeeze, runs to her room as she sheever.

But the debauchery Manudev looked at her residing off, lustfully and became adament to "own" her.

His lascivious lips gives out a shigh as a tiger gives out on missing the flesh of the deer.....

Dreamy Nightmare

Amrapali, in the meantime whereof,
Had a childhood love
By the name of Pushpakumar thereof.
They were deeply in love with each other,
Even planned to wed each other.
Not wanting to lose Amrapali,
Manudev killed Pushpakumar on the day of their wedding before it can go through evenly.
Wanting to possess her completely,
He then declared that Amrapali would be the "bride of Vaishali",
That is, the Nagarvadhu.
By the name of, "Vaishali's Janpath Kalyani," henceforth for seven year Amrapali would be regarded to.
In accordance with the wish of that salacious balmy,
Janapath Kalyani and Nagarbadhu becomes the fate of dreamy incubus for Amrapaali.

Janpath Kalyani- the most beautiful and talented girl in the kingdom. This post of Janpath Kalyani would last for seven years for amraplai. During this period, she had the right to choose her lover and also choose the person with whom she wished to maintain physical relations....

Nagarvadhu- Bride of the city.

A pure heart doused in clart

It's truly said that a pure heart,
Is always filled with love even when being doused in clart.
That was so true for Amrapali,
She was always thinking of making othe's life better trying to paint their life beautifully,
Even during her life's unwished catastrophe wholly.
Along with Janpath Kalyani she also remained the court dancer of the Vaishali's democracy,
She thus tried to help the needy by playing tricks of provocacy.
She used it to lure of the courtesans, the lust-filled blatters,
And always tried of making the life of desolate and helpless women and girls better.

Love knows no boundary

Tales of her beauty and talent
Soon reached very wide even to the far end.
King Bimbisara, ruler of the neighboring hostile Magadha region,
Was enamored by these stories and wished to see her and befriend.
It was God's grace or destiny's play rather,
The two kingdoms waged a war against each other.
While attacking Vaishali Bimbisar got injured heavily
Thus took refuge in very own residence of Amrapali.
Bimbisar was an excellent musician and would often sing to her.
In due course of time, the two fell deeply in love with each other.
But it was only a few weeks before Amrapali learned of Bimbisara's true identity.
Angered, she asked him to call off the war and leave immediately.
Totally smitten by Amrapali,
Bimbisara readily agreed to every wishes she hurled hurriedly.
He did not even care that it made him seem like a coward
In the eyes of the residents of Vaishali and the world.
In the next few months, Amrapali bore him a son like a shinning ratna,
Who she named,'Vimala Kondanna'.

Do father's love can ever be shoved off?

Years have slipped by, in the game of throne and in time's string.
Ajatashatru has imprisoned his father Bimbisar and has declared himself the king.
Ajatshatru kept on tormenting his father in prison.
He ordered that Bimbisara be given no food and also tortured him physically, injuring his body in the imprison.
Queen Kosala devi kept finding different ways of reaching food to him in his living-grave,very silent.
However, when she was caught, she was altogether stopped from visiting her husband.
Bimbisara gradually started growing weak, but derived comfort by looking at a distant mountain from his cell window.
The mountain was than inhabited by Gautama Buddha and it rang with his disciples outflow.
When Ajatashatru realized his father's enjoys-lark,
he ordered his people to block the window and make his room dark.
One day, Buddha and his disciples was in the city tour.
An overjoyed Bimbisara got to see him through the holes of his prison door.
Incensed that his father got a chance to be happy again,

Ajatashatru ordered his henchmen to skin his feet with a burning chain.

After this incident, Bimbisara could no longer move around.

Ultimately, he kept getting weaker and weaker and even his breath was about to loose his sound.

But finally a day of suprise evie,

Ajatashatru was sharing a meal with his mother, Kosala Devi.

Ajatashatru having his meal with the rest of the family,

Holding his newborn son on his lap clammily.

He proudly asked his mother, Kosala Devi,"Have you ever seen a devoted father as I am??"

Several incidents from his childhood, where his father had showered all his love and devotion on his son, his mother narrates there and.

An emotional and guilty Ajatashatru immediately decided that he would free his father from imprison.

He hurried to the dungeon with an axe, in order to cut open his chains and let's father free in barbizon.

When Bimbisara saw his son approaching him with an axe, he misread the situation and thought that he was going to slit him sharp.

Not wanting to die at his son's hands, he decided to take his own life up,

By consuming the talaputa poison present in his ring like death's honey syrup.

But still before closing his eyes for the last time he mumbled his last prayer for eudaemonia of his son, almost immediately his weak breath gave up....

Love for motherland is even bigger than love for self and respect

Ajatashatru repented much for the loss of his father.
However, none of it was of any use then and after.
Finally, he moved to Champa,improved all its facilities,
And made that city his principle metropolis.
But soon after his father's death,
Ajatashatru decided to invade all the enemy capitals around Magadha with his dreadful legions.
He then waged war against Vajji, which was then ruled by the Lichchhavis, also conquering Vaishali, Kosala, Kashi and many other neighboring regions.
In the other hand time has played an unique game with Amrapali,
With age instead of her beauty being grazed off it's bloom gazed as the lily.
Having conquered Vaishali, Ajatashatru was one-day roaming the streets in triumph of war.
He had heard much about Amrapali and wished to be an audience with her.
A short search led him to her residence.
Seeing her, he immediately fell for her beauty and charm like his

father and it never seemed like an coincidence.
She too liked his brutish-dove
And, gradually begun to reciprocate to his love.
The jealous residents of Vaishali, however, were against Amrapali's relationship sinuous.
Demanded that Amrapali be imprisoned for her promiscuous.
Seeing her imprisoned and helpless, Ajatshatru became so upset that he burned down the whole of Vaishali. Several hundreds of people died in the huge massacre and the city was almost completely ruined,but he saw all the way through out towards the safety of his love, Amrapali.
When she comes out of his apprehend,
She was aggrieved seeing the amount of damage the invasion had caused to her motherland.
Disgusted with Ajatashatru, she walked away from him for good.
Even though Amrapali never knew that Ajatashatru was her lover's son, standing afoot;
Or that he had killed his own father,
Who was also her own child's dad too....

Some story shell from times dwell

Time has ran it's course.
Ajatashatru eventually became the monarch of a vast kingdom of multitude source.
It spanned almost all areas of present-day North India, including Chandigarh, Uttarakhand, Bihar, Himachal Pradesh, Uttar Pradesh, Delhi, Chhattisgarh, West Bengal, a bit of Jharkhand and a fourth of Madhya Pradesh as well.
Ajatashatru considered to be one of the most powerful rulers North India in the time's dwell.
With the help of his two ministers, Sunidha and Vassakaara, he built a massive fort by the banks of the Ganga,
In order to further strengthen the security of Magadha.
He named this place Paatali Grama, which later became popular as Pataliputra.
When Pataliputra was being built,
Gautam Buddha happened to pass through it's silt.
He praised the city for its beauty,
However pointed out that three things could prove detrimental to the city.
Namely, water, fire and general discord amongst the people living there,

And as in the measure of time all this three things one time or the other had been the cause of Patliputra's despair.

Pataliputra-mordern day Patna.

Too much of sense of the outer world is bit of nonsense

One fine day.
Young prince of Kaushambi comes to Buddha to become his follower and to get over the life's dismay.
The young prince have came to Buddha with the wish to become Sanyashi.
So Buddha sends him for alms to the house of an young Sadhika far from the cities ecstacy.
The Rajputra went to the Sadhika's homestead.
While he reached the house, the young Sadhika welcomes him,very glad indeed.
She makes him seat.
Some thoughts started sailing in the prince's head as fleet.
He was thinking, now as he has become Sanyashi he will not get those delicious food that he loves,
Instead he would have to eat any food that he gets.
As, he was just thinking, that, ok for him now it have to be fine,
The Sadhika serves all the delicacies that he loved in a plater filled of delicious nine.
He can't believe it,he thought,"really!is this true realy!",
He eat the food very heartily.
After the food he started perciving,

That till yesterday after having his food he used to rest in his palace for few revving.

But from today, he has become Sanyashi,

He will have to walk back in the sun and can't be a lazy-shasy.

Suddenly the Sadhika says out,"It's too hot outside please rest for a bit, before you walk back."

The prince was surprised but he thought it as a coincidence,and nothing as such a hack.

Probably the girl have thought the same,that he is a young boy just becoming sadhu, in this sun who has to walk some feets,

So he should rest for a bit till the sun downs his heat by some mercury beeds.

The prince laid down, his mind started sparking,

That now as he has left his previous life behind without meandering.

Now he has no hand of father to protect him or a roof to shelther except the natures behest.

Suddenly the Sadhika who was going back after laying the carpet for him to take some rest.

She turned back and said, "Hey,Bhranta, why are you saying this, there can be no protector better than Mahatma Buddha, no roof as strong as the sky and no bed as beautiful as the ground."

The prince jumps up with a jolt he is now quite confident this can't be coincidence of any more round.

So he asked the sadhika, "Dear, can you read my mind?"

The Sadhika says with a short smile, "Yaha I can read the minds
there in front of me,there thoughts intertwined"
The prince suprised with a wide open mouth, "But how?"
The Sadhika says, "First I started by reading my own thoughts,
That use to rise up in my mind and all waves that hit my soul like
unruly rocks.
But slowly slowly it started drying up.
My whole inside became very calm, almost numb,
Now generaly no waves disturbs my mind,
It's now not disturbed by presumption's ruffling wind,
Since than I can read the thoughts of other's mind."
Listening this the prince stood up and started on his return track.
On reaching Buddha he says, "To that sadhika's house,I will never
go back."
Buddha, "Why?were you were ill-treated by her??"
The prince,"No,no, infact I was welcomed heartily and greeted
very warmly by her."
Buddha,"You did something wrong?"
The prince, "No,not that,actually the sadhika can read minds
Thoughts of person in front of her, she can find.
When I entered the room seeing her so beautiful
My mind also got strayed in the concupiscence pool.
She has surely read that too,isn't that awful.
So, I can't face her anymore,for my part, it's so shameful."
Buddha, "No you have to go to her house,

That will be your sadhana to rouse.
Go to her house, fully conscious reading every thought that comes to your mind now and then,
Be fully awake but don't try to supprass any thought that cross your mind,just read them."
Next day again the prince was walking to the Sadhika's house.
He is trying to be fully conscious being,
He can read every thought that's crossing his brain strain,
He can feel a diya is burning inside his heart making himself very clear from within.
He can read and understand his every thought,
It has never been in the past although this is what he has always sought,
His brain has been so awakeningly ought.
As he nears the house he can feel that he is becoming more and more calm within,
It feels his inside has become so calm that he can hear the sound of even the fall of a pin."
Slowly as he enters the house his thoughts started drying up and the soul started becoming calm and calm. No more waves of thoughts are inside him, he have his food and took rest, inside him there was no qualm. He returned to Buddha dancing on his way back,
While his whole face is enlightened under the light of calmness and knowledge's crack.

Returning to Buddha he fell flat-on Buddha's feet and started crying.

Buddha pulled him up and asked, "Son,what was your today's feeling ??"

The prince started slowly, "Today it was a very surprising experience,

As I was nearing the Sadhika's house my heart started becoming calm and calm with no indulgence,

The waves of thought started drying up,the whole around me semmed filled in indifference.

I became fully awaken from within.

Than as I went before the sadhika,by then all waves of thought has dried up leaving back nothing.

There was complete silence inside me,

My conscience was in its peak as I felt myself free."

Buddha smiled and said,"You have attained success in your sadhana,

From tomorrow you don't have to go to her house you have put your first step towards nirvana.

Always keep this consciousness that you have learnt,

Let this enlightment always burn inside you, that tody you have earned.

Always be waken-up from within.

Remember the path of ultimate and eternal happiness reside inside our very being.

Sanyashi is a person who is fully conscious,
Wakened up from within in all awarness.
That's what enlightment or nirvana the ultimate path of eternal bliss and happiness.
As you have engraved in that path,so, from today you will be called "Anand",which means happiness".

- *Sadhana- disciplined and dedicated practice or learning.*

- *Nirvana-Sense of ultimate peace and happiness giving up all materilstic desires.*

The seductive spirituality

Few months have slipped by.
One day as Buddha with his disciples was walking by.
Amrapali spotted Anand from her terrace,
She was immediately tranced by the calmness and the light of knowledge that glowed on his face.
Amrapali thus fall for him.
For a meal she invited them, but also requested him,
To stay on for the next four months further,
Till the ongoing monsoon season got over.
Sworn to a life of celibacy,
Anand replied that he could ony agree to her efficacy,
If Buddha gave him permission to this arbitary.
The other young Bhikkhsus of Buddha's retinue came to know of this affinity,
They became jealous of Anand, and before Buddha, against him, they started putting some anti-advocacy .
It clearly showed for many nirvana is a very far road to reach as they are still being entangled by jealousy.
They reached the news to the Buddha's ear,
Much before this Anand could request an audience with him on this matter.
The other monks were hoping that the Buddha would become angry and throw him out of the order.

But,Buddha smiled and gave Anand permission to stay at Amrapali's residence,to everyone's wonder . Anand stayed there for four months, as was required of him.

Everyone was convinced that between this time's brim,

Anand would have had a physical relationship with her it seem.

After the said time period elapsed into the shadow,

Anand returned to the monastery, with a saffron-clad Amrapali in tow.

Everyone was suprised,but Buddha smiled,

It's much what he had expected.

Anand had successfully converted her into a Bhikkhuni.

"I tried to seduce Anand many times, but had utterly failed in all my attempts",said Amrapali.

"In the end, he had spiritually seduced me; making me renounce my pointless materialistic world.

And hence I am here trying to find a sollace in Buddha's feet and join his monk order."

Questioning Buddha,"Why not?"

Amrapali requested Buddha to take her into his Sangha as a Bhikkhuni.
Initially, Buddha refused to grant her the wish,making her bit gloomy.
Buddha says,"Only Bhikkhus are in the Sanghas therein,
And that there is no arrangement for Bhikkhunis to join in."
Amrapali shakes of the mark of the quick nerves,
And boldly questioned her stand with utmost impulse.
Buddha patiently tried to explain that a woman could end up tempting the Bhikkhus,
Making them break their vow of celibacy,thus.
Amrapali hotly debated that as well,
Saying that if the monks were spiritually strong enough like the stringent ell,
And if Buddha had confidence on them as he had on Anand,will they ever out bell??.
How could they be swayed by a mere woman,
And if they are swayed by a mere woman will not they be swayed too by worlds all other luxary cushion.
Than would they be pure from the encephalon and the soul,
Or wouldn't it just be a mask of control,

And no steps in the path of consciousness at all or nirvana in whole.
Finally, Buddha had to give in to her wishes and wits,
And into his fold Buddha let Amrapali admits.
In due course of time, Amrapali, who became deeply involved with the Dhamma and the Sangha,
Achieved enlightenment and remained as one of the main disciples of the Buddha.
She was also posted as the head of the Bhikkhuni Sangha.
A few years later, her son Vimala Kondanna,
Too joined the order and became a Buddhist monk and was named Kaundinya.

- *Bhikkhus*-An ardent male Buddhist monasticism.
- *Bhikkhunis*- An ardent female Buddhist monasticism.

Denouement

In the meantime Ajatashatru also got closely associated with the Buddha.
After repenting for all his deeds in times prelude a,
He completely surrendered himself to the Buddha, the Dhammas and the Sangha.
He became an avid follower of the Buddha and even erected a massive Stupa,
After the funeral of Buddha,built on the bones and ashes of the Buddha.
Further, he was also present at the first Buddhist council at the Sattapanni (Saptaparni) caves, Rajgir.
Amrapali also died in times ager,
Anand went on his journey of spreading the teachings of Buddha and his abler.
While Ajatashatru was brutally killed by his own son Uddyabhadra.
Thus time played his flute of indementia.
As Ajatashatru tortured his father,
So was he killed by his own son there after.
Finally, what remained in time were ther insignia,
And the mango garden of Amrapali that she donated in Buddha's order,the Ambapali vana,
Here, Buddha preached the famous Ambapalika Sutta......

34. Life as Life

Life is a mirage of beauty,
Ruined in vanity,
And lots of sentimental intensity.
Never fall for blarney activity,
Sometime the best thing in life is conscious-passivity....

35. Drizzle of love

Villages are the beautiful libraries of love where emotions are indorsed there of,
Where as the cities are the grand market where emotions are bargained of...

She shattered my heart into so many pieces,
That collecting those pieces made life an accident...

Faithfulness once asked faithlessness, "Why do you break hearts?"
Faithlessness answered with a smile, "In faithfulness of love the life shouldn't go a loss,I save the heart from it"...

The syllables the devotee puts in his prayer for the almighty lord,
In the same verse the lord replies...

I want to fall head-on in love with just one honey,
And not have the time or interest of playing the game of heart with butterflies many...

It started so so small, "I like you",
But now it is so immense, "I don't love anyone else, love less mysel too"...

Even the diamond thinks itself to be only a stone,
When can it itself calculate and have its own value known .....

There had been a time when I even believed in magic and miracle,
And now this is the time when even the truth of reality seems just an obsolete bunch of satire...

Friends don't be so proud of the looks or colour of this mortal body,
It's final destination is to convert to ash or to soil...

Don't try searching someone other in someone other,
First find yourself in you...

Everyone of us now a days read millions of book to reside in peace,
But most of us don't try to read the soul that resides inside us and is the crafter of that ultimate peace....

36. Last song of swan

Beauty has its ugly sides,
Genius is a spice of creative madness,
Intellect is a burden,
Ignorance a bliss riden,
While half knowledge create perception,
That we love through our grey lens and insane.
We try making things that we perceive to be simply dark and white,
But is it always true?? is it always that simple wrong and right??
We just support a side and not ready to hear the voice of the other,
We forget it's time who plays it's drama rather altogether,
We are only just characters of it for certain,
Thats bound to bite the dust when time rolls down its curtain,
And when the drama of time ends only thing that remains is the time and it's perception,
And only and only the time and it's perception.....

Random Thoughts,why?

I have end by writing a running commentary about Amrapali's esse whereof,
I felt that all my poems some how related to her thereof.
She has reached the ultimate servitude in love.
Going out of the dungeons of senses,
To ultimate height of consciousness.
A journey from beauty's grandeur magnitude to sainthood,
It's a beautiful story of sacrifice, renouncement, love and ultimately self realisation to be understood,
That had larked me throught out my life and a story through the time it had stood.
I didn't tried to make it an illusive poetry like my Guru Ramdhari has done in Urvashi
As still I have not been able to pluck the lotus from the pond washy.
So I thought I would not be able to justify to mata Amrapali.
Thus I have just put on a running commentary,
Before ending my book, hope you all also enjoy the solitary.
I will end it up with just one say.
That this book is compilation of few of my poems taken out as raw as prgvossible from my dairies,
Filled with beguiling crude emotions.....

Thanking Note

I am thankful to every reader for bearing with me. Please put your reviews about my poems, from wherever you buy it and wherever possible. I would love to listen from you all and try to improve. You can also reach up to me,in my mail id: kuntalghosh1@gmail.com.

Printed by Libri Plureos GmbH in Hamburg,
Germany